CW01559123

Native American Cookbook of Modern & Traditional Recipes

Celebrating the Culture of America's Indigenous People

Copyright Material

Sign-up Now
and Be Notified of New Books

Website: readbooks.today

Table of Contents

MAIN DISHES   36

DESSERTS   61

Drinks

Cedar-Maple Tea

Prep Time: 10 minutes
Cooking Time: 20 minutes
Servings: 01

Ingredients

- 1 cup packed cedar, chopped
- ½ tablespoon maple syrup/honey or ½ teaspoon of Stevia
- 2 ½ to 3 cups spring water

Directions

1. Add cedar and water to a pot; place it over moderate heat until water begins to boil. Once done; decrease the heat to medium low & let simmer for 10 minutes.
2. Once the color changes to golden brown, tea is ready. Turn off the heat & strain the tea over a large pot or bowl using a strainer. Let the sediment to settle in the pot or bowl for a couple of seconds. Pour the tea into a teacup & let it settle for a couple of seconds. Add the honey or maple syrup; give it a good stir.

Juniper Tea

Prep Time: 05 minutes
Cooking Time: 20 minutes
Servings: 01

Ingredients

- 1 teaspoon juniper berries, dried
- 1 ½ cups boiling water
- 1 teaspoon honey

Directions

1. Add the juniper berries to a tea ball & place in a large mug.
2. Pour the boiling water carefully into the mug. Let steep for a couple of minutes. Strain the berries. Add the honey; give it a good stir.

Sassafras Tea

Prep Time: 10 minutes
Cooking Time: 20 minutes
Servings: 05

Ingredients

- Honey or maple syrup for serving
- 1 thin slice of fresh ginger
- A small handful of sassafras roots, thoroughly washed in cold water
- ½ cinnamon stick
- Sparkling water

Directions

1. Chop up the sassafras roots using a heavy knife or pound them with the handle until you could smell their spicy scent. Place the roots in a saucepan with 6 cups of water and the cinnamon; bring the mix to a boil, over moderate heat. Once done; decrease the heat & let simmer for 20 minutes, partially covered. Add the ginger & let simmer for 2 more minutes.
2. Line a fine-mesh strainer with a coffee filter & place it over a bowl. Pour the tea through. Sweeten with honey or maple syrup to taste. Drink hot and enjoy.

Sumac Lemonade

Prep Time: 10 minutes
Cooking Time: 20 minutes
Servings: 08

Ingredients

For Sumac Syrup:
- 2 cups water
- 3 tablespoons ground sumac
- 2 cups sugar

For Soda:
- 1 tablespoon juice from 1 lemon, plus 1 lemon, cut into wedges
- ¼ cup sumac syrup
- 1 cup seltzer or club soda

Directions

1. For Sumac Syrup: Over moderate heat in a small saucepan; combine the sugar with water until the sugar is completely dissolved, stirring occasionally. Let cool to room temperature. Once done; add the sumac; give it a good stir until mixed well and let infuse for a couple of minutes. Strain through a fine mesh strainer.
2. For Soda: Combine 1 cup of club soda with 1 tablespoon of lemon juice, and ¼ cup of sumac syrup in a cup for each serving. Add ice; give it a good stir. Serve immediately with some lemon wedges and enjoy.

Soups & Salads

Wild Gitigan Salad

Prep Time: 20 minutes
Cooking Time: 30 minutes
Servings: 04

Ingredients

For Salad:
- 4 sprigs of fresh thyme
- 1 cup black beans, cooked
- 3 cups vegetable broth, low sodium
- 1½ cups whole wild rice
- 2 bunches kale (approximately 8 cups)
- ½ cup Parmesan cheese or pecorino Romano cheese, grated
- 1 cup ground cherries or baby tomatoes, rinsed & halved

For Dressing:
- Juice of 1 lemon (approximately 2 tablespoons)
- ¼ cup extra virgin olive oil
- 1 tablespoon lemon zest, freshly grated
- ¼ teaspoon each of freshly ground black pepper & salt

Directions

1. Soak the beans for overnight and then, add the beans to a pot of fresh water; boil for 1 to 2 hours, until done. Set aside to cool.
2. Prepare the wild rice. Rinse the rice well in a bowl of cold water; drain well. Add rice, thyme, and vegetable broth to a pot & let simmer per the directions mentioned on the package, for 20 minutes. Remove from the heat & let the rice stand in the pot for 5 minutes, covered. Remove the thyme stems & fluff the rice well using a fork. Set aside to cool.
3. Wash the kale & remove the ribs. Once done; slice the kale thinly into ribbons. Spin using a salad spinner until most of the water is absorbed.
4. Add the kale, a drizzle of olive oil, and a bit of salt in a large serving bowl. Massage the kale for 2 to 3 minutes, until it begins to soften & wilt; set aside while you prepare the dressing.
5. For Dressing: Whisk the lemon zest with lemon juice, ¼ cup of olive oil, and pepper & salt in a small-sized mixing bowl until mixed well.
6. To serve, add the wild rice followed by cooked black beans, ground cherries or tomatoes, and sprinkle with the cheese. Drizzle the dressing on top; gently toss to combine. Serve and enjoy

Three Sisters Soup

Prep Time: 20 minutes
Cooking Time: 30 minutes
Servings: 06

Ingredients

- 2 cups butternut squash, peeled & cubed
- 5 cups water
- 2 cups canned yellow or white hominy, drained
- 1 ½ cups potatoes, peeled & diced
- 2 tablespoons all-purpose flour
- 1 ½ tablespoons chicken bouillon granules
- 2 tablespoons melted butter
- ¼ teaspoon pepper
- 2 cups fresh green beans, trimmed & snapped

Directions

1. Place the green beans with hominy, potatoes, and squash into a pot; pour in chicken bouillon and water. Bring the mix to a boil. Once done; decrease the heat to low & let simmer for 10 minutes, until the vegetables are soft. Blend flour into the butter and then, stir into the prepared soup. Increase the heat to medium & cook until soup thickens, for 5 minutes more. Season with pepper; serve and enjoy.

Chicken, Corn & Chili Soup

Prep Time: 30 minutes
Cooking Time: 30 minutes
Servings: 18

Ingredients

- 1 ¾ pounds chicken breast meat, diced
- 1 can tomato sauce (15 ounce)
- 2 red bell peppers, diced
- ½ cup corn kernels, frozen
- 4 cans kidney beans with liquid (15 ounce each)
- 1 onion, diced
- 2 cans diced tomatoes (14.5 ounce each)
- 1 tablespoon dried parsley
- 2 green bell peppers, diced
- 1 teaspoon garlic powder
- 2 teaspoons chili powder
- ½ teaspoon ground cayenne pepper
- 2 cups water
- ½ teaspoon ground cumin

Directions

1. Coat a large pot lightly with the cooking spray & place it over moderate heat. Cook & stir the chicken with onion and bell peppers until the peppers are just tender and chicken is brown.
2. Stir in the beans, corn, tomatoes, tomato sauce & water. Season with parsley, chili powder, garlic powder, cumin, and cayenne. Decrease the heat; cover & let simmer for half an hour.

Algonquin Nut Soup

Prep Time: 40 minutes
Cooking Time: 60 minutes
Servings: 06

Ingredients

- 24 ounces hazelnuts, crushed
- 6 cups chicken stock or venison stock
- 3 tablespoons parsley, chopped
- 6 shallots, with tops
- ¼ teaspoon black pepper
- 1 teaspoon salt

Directions

1. Place all the ingredients together in a large soup pot & let simmer for 1 ½ hours, over medium heat, stirring now and then.

Dry Meat Soup

Prep Time: 10 minutes
Cooking Time: 1 hour & 30 minutes
Servings: 04

Ingredients

- Salt pork
- Dry meat
- Potatoes or hominy
- Water, as needed

Directions

1. Fill a large sauce pan with water; bring it to a boil and then, add the dry meat. Cook until the meat turns soft, for a couple of hours.
2. Once the meat turns soft, add the hominy or potatoes and salt pork.
3. Bring the soup to a boil. Decrease the heat to medium and continue to cook until the leftover ingredients are cooked through.

Pozole

Prep Time: 30 minutes
Cooking Time: 3 hours & 20 minutes
Servings: 08

Ingredients

- 3-pound pork shoulder, cut into 2" pieces
- 1 large yellow onion, quartered
- 3 garlic cloves, sliced
- 1 teaspoon whole cloves
- 4 cups chicken broth, low sodium
- 1 teaspoon cumin seeds
- 2 dried guajillo chiles, stem & seeds removed
- 1 bay leaf
- 3 (15-ounces) cans hominy, drained & rinsed
- 2 dried chiles de arbol, stem & seeds removed
- Freshly ground black pepper & kosher salt to taste
- 2 dried ancho chiles, stem & seeds removed

For Serving:
- Freshly chopped cilantro
- Thinly sliced green cabbage
- Thinly sliced radishes

Directions

1. Season the pork with pepper and salt to taste. Next, over moderate heat in a large pot; add the pork with onion, garlic, cumin seeds, cloves, broth, and bay leaf.
2. Add water (enough to cover the meat by 2"). Bring it to a boil, over moderate heat. Cover & decrease the heat; let simmer for 1 ½ hours, removing the foam appearing on top, as needed.
3. Place the chilies into a medium-sized mixing bowl; pour 2 cups of boiling water on top and let soak for half an hour.
4. Place the chilies and ½ cup of their soaking liquid into a blender. Blend until completely smooth; feel free to add more of water as needed.
5. Add the chile puree & hominy to pot with pork. Continue to simmer for 1 hour & 30 more minutes, until pork is very tender, covered.
6. Serve the pozole with cabbage, radishes, and cilantro.

Breads & More

Blue Corn Stuffing

Prep Time: 10 minutes
Cooking Time: 30 minutes
Servings: 08

Ingredients

- 1 pound bulk Italian sausage or bulk chorizo sausage
- ½ cup carrot, chopped
- 1 cup celery, chopped
- 4 fresh Serrano or jalapeno peppers, seeded & finely chopped
- 1 medium onion, chopped (approximately ½ cup)
- ½ teaspoon dried thyme, crushed
- 4 garlic cloves, minced
- ½ teaspoon dried sage, crushed
- 6 cup Blue Corn Bread, coarsely crumbled
- ½ cup chicken broth

For Blue Corn Bread
- 2 garlic cloves, minced
- ¼ cup butter or margarine
- 2 tablespoon sugar
- 1 ½ cup yellow or blue cornmeal
- 2 large eggs
- 1 tablespoon baking powder
- ½ cup all-purpose flour
- 1 cup milk
- ½ teaspoon salt

Directions

1. Over moderate heat in a large skillet; cook the sausage with onion, celery, carrot, garlic, and peppers until the sausage turns brown & vegetables are tender, for 10 minutes. Drain the fat off and immediately stir in the sage and thyme.
2. Next, stir the crumbled corn bread with sausage mixture in a large-sized mixing bowl. Add broth, gently toss to moisten. Use to stuff one 8 to 10 pounds turkey. Spoon any stuffing that doesn't fit into the turkey into a casserole. Cover & let chill. Bake during the last 30 minutes of roasting, covered.

For Blue Corn Bread

1. Over moderate heat in a small skillet; cook butter or margarine and garlic for a minute or two, until garlic turns tender. Next, stir the cornmeal with baking powder, flour, sugar, and salt in a medium-sized mixing bowl. Stir the eggs with milk, and margarine-garlic mixture in a separate medium-sized mixing bowl. Add to the cornmeal mixture. Stir until the batter is just smooth. Pour into a greased, large baking pan. Bake until a wooden toothpick comes out clean, for 20 to 25 minutes, at 425 F. Let cool on a wire rack in the pan.

Acorn Bread

Prep Time: 20 minutes
Cooking Time: 50 minutes
Servings: 08

Ingredients

- 1 cup acorn meal
- 2 tablespoons baking powder
- 1 cup soy or rice milk
- 3 tablespoons sugar
- 1 beaten egg, or 1 egg substitute
- 3 tablespoons oil
- 1 cup flour
- ½ teaspoon salt

Directions

1. Preheat your oven to 400F.
2. Grease a large loaf pan.
3. Sift all the dry ingredients together in a large bowl.
4. Combine the egg with milk & oil in a separate bowl.
5. Combine all the liquid and dry ingredients; give the ingredients a good stir until the dry ingredients are just moistened.
6. Pour into a greased pan & bake for 30 minutes at 400 F.
7. Examine the acorns as you pick and throw away any that are wormy/ cracked / moldy /etc.
8. Next, shell them.
9. Taste the raw acorns (if taste bitter); boil them, if needed.
10. The acorns are ready; when the water no longer turns brown (looks like tea).
11. Next slightly roast the acorns in a warm oven, at 250 F.
12. Once roasted, you can use the acorns in place of nuts in many recipes. You can even glaze like chestnuts, simmered in a soup, ground, and used as a flour extender.

Bannock

Prep Time: 10 minutes
Cooking Time: 30 minutes
Servings: 12

Ingredients

- 3 cups all-purpose flour
- ¼ cup butter, melted
- 2 tablespoons baking powder
- 1 ½ cups water
- 1 teaspoon salt

Directions

1. Stir the flour with baking powder & salt in a large-sized mixing bowl until mixed well. Pour melted butter and water on top of the flour mixture. Give it a good stir using a large fork to create a ball.
2. Turn out the dough onto a lightly floured surface; gently knead for 10 times. Pat into a flat circle, approximately ¾ to 1" thick.
3. Warm a greased frying pan over moderate heat.
4. Place the dough in the hot pan & cook for 15 minutes on each side, until browned. For easy turning, feel free to use two lifters.

Pumpkin Blue Cornbread

Prep Time: 20 minutes
Cooking Time: 20 minutes
Servings: 10

Ingredients

For Cornbread:
- 1 cup yellow cornmeal
- ½ cup sour cream
- 1 cup all-purpose flour
- ¼ teaspoon ground nutmeg
- 1 tablespoon baking powder
- ¼ cup butter, melted
- 1 teaspoon ground cinnamon
- ½ teaspoon baking soda
- 1 cup pumpkin puree
- ⅓ cup brown sugar
- 2 large eggs
- ¾ teaspoon salt

For Whipped Honey Butter:
- 2 tablespoons honey
- ½ cup softened butter
- 1 teaspoon salt
- ¼ teaspoon ground cinnamon

Directions

1. Lightly coat a 9" square baking dish with the cooking spray and then, preheat your oven to 400F. Next, whisk the cornmeal with flour, cinnamon, baking powder, baking soda, nutmeg, and salt in a large-sized mixing bowl until mixed well.

2. Whisk the pumpkin puree with sour cream, melted butter, and brown sugar in a separate medium-sized mixing bowl until completely smooth. Slowly add the eggs; beat well after each addition. Pour this mix on top of the dry ingredients; give it a good stir until just mixed.

3. Spread the prepared batter into the baking dish & bake for 20 minutes, until a toothpick comes out clean. Let completely cool before slicing into desired squares.

4. Whip the butter with honey, cinnamon, and salt in a medium-sized mixing bowl until completely fluffy. Serve with the cornbread.

Frybread

Prep Time: 10 minutes
Cooking Time: 10 minutes
Servings: 04

Ingredients

- 1 cup all-purpose flour, plus additional for dusting
- ½ cup milk
- 3 cups vegetable oil or shortening
- 1 ½ teaspoons baking powder
- ¼ teaspoon salt

Directions

1. Fill a deep, heavy saucepan or large cast-iron skillet with 1" of oil and place it over moderate heat until hot.
2. In the meantime, combine the flour with baking powder & salt in a large bowl until mixed well
3. Add the milk; give it a good stir until the dough holds together.
4. Knead on a floured surface for 3 or 4 times.
5. Evenly divide the dough into 4 pieces; shaping each into a ball.
6. Roll each ball dough into a ¼ to ½" thick circle using a lightly floured rolling pin. Make a depression in middle of each round of dough.
7. Carefully slide 1 or 2 pieces of formed dough into the hot oil. Fry until browned lightly, for a minute or two per side.
8. Remove the fried dough to paper towels to drain. Just before serving; sprinkle the fried bread with a bit of sugar and cinnamon. Enjoy.

Fried Cornbread

Prep Time: 20 minutes
Cooking Time: 20 minutes
Servings: 10

Ingredients

- 2 teaspoons baking powder
- 1 cup self-rising flour
- ¾ cup buttermilk
- 1 cup all-purpose cornmeal
- ¼ cup bacon drippings or cooking oil
- 2 large eggs, beaten
- ⅓ cup water
- 1 tablespoon butter
- ½ teaspoon salt
- 1 tablespoon sugar, optional

Directions

1. Line a large, rimmed baking sheet with the paper towels & place a rack on top; set aside.
2. Next, whisk the flour with baking powder, cornmeal, sugar, and salt in a medium-sized mixing bowl until mixed well.
3. Add buttermilk, eggs, and water; mix well.
4. Now, over moderate heat in a cast iron skillet; heat the butter and oil. Once done; drop the prepared batter carefully into the hot skillet to form small medallions (approximately ⅛ cup measure).
5. Fry until crisp and brown; turn & cook until brown on the other side as well. Remove & let drain on the rack.
6. Serve immediately with honey butter or warm syrup for breakfast. Enjoy

Masa Polenta

Prep Time: 20 minutes
Cooking Time: 30 minutes
Servings: 04

Ingredients

- 5 ounces parmesan cheese, finely shredded
- 2/3 cup whole milk
- 1 ⅓ cups chicken broth
- ¾ cup masa harina or yellow cornmeal
- 2 tablespoons unsalted butter
- ½ teaspoon black pepper

Directions

1. Bring the chicken broth & milk to a boil in a large saucepan, over moderate heat.
2. Slowly whisk in the cornmeal.
3. Cover & let simmer until creamy, for 20 minutes, stirring now and then; ensure it doesn't stick to the bottom.
4. Remove from the heat & stir in the butter followed by black pepper.
5. Slowly stir in the cheese until completely melted.
6. Serve immediately and enjoy.

Vegetables

Succotash

Prep Time: 30 minutes
Cooking Time: 1 hour & 20 minutes
Servings: 04

Ingredients

- 4 center-cut bacon slices
- 10 ounces baby lima beans, fresh or frozen
- 4 ounces fresh okra, cut into ½" thick slices
- 1 cup sweet onion, chopped
- 3 cups fresh corn kernels
- 1 garlic clove, finely chopped
- 3 tablespoons butter
- ¼ cup fresh basil, thinly sliced
- 5 ounces cherry tomatoes, halved
- ¼ teaspoon black pepper
- 1 ¼ teaspoons kosher salt

Directions

1. Fill a medium saucepan with water (enough to cover the lima beans). Once done; add the beans and bring it to a boil, over moderate heat. Decrease the heat to medium-low & let simmer for 8 to 10 minutes, until beans are just tender. Drain & set aside.
2. While the beans simmer, place the slices of bacon over medium heat in a large cast-iron skillet. Cook for 8 minutes, until crisp; turning once halfway. Transfer the bacon to paper towels; crumble & set aside. Reserve the drippings in skillet.
3. Add fresh okra, chopped onion, and garlic to the same skillet and cook over moderate heat for 6 minutes, until onion is just tender, stirring often. Stir in the fresh corn kernels, drained beans, pepper, and salt. Cook for 5 to 7 minutes, until corn is bright yellow and tender, stirring often. Add butter & cook for a minute, until butter is melted, stirring constantly. Remove from the heat.
4. Stir in the halved cherry tomatoes & sliced basil; sprinkle with the crumbled bacon; serve immediately and enjoy.

Wild Rice with Root Vegetables

Prep Time: 10 minutes
Cooking Time: 1 hour & 10 minutes
Servings: 04

Ingredients

- 1 cup wild rice, rinsed well
- ¼ cup dried cranberries
- 1 medium carrot, cut into 1" pieces
- ¼ cup plus 1 tablespoon extra-virgin olive oil, divided
- 1 medium sweet potato, cut into ½" pieces
- ¼ cup vinegar
- 1 tablespoon maple syrup
- 1 purple potato, cut into ½" pieces
- Freshly ground black pepper & kosher salt to taste
- 1 medium red onion, sliced

Directions

1. Preheat your oven to 375F.
2. Next, over moderate heat in a medium saucepan; combine the wild rice with 3 cups of cold water. Cover & bring it to a boil.
3. Once done; decrease the heat to a simmer & cook for 40 to 45 minutes, until rice is split and tender. Drain & transfer to a large-sized mixing bowl.
4. In the meantime, roast the vegetables. Toss the vegetables with 1 tablespoon of olive oil & spread on a large-sized baking sheet in an even layer. Season with pepper and salt; roast for 25 to 30 minutes, until tender.
5. Combine the dried cranberries with maple syrup, and vinegar in a blender & pulse until ingredients are mixed well. Slowly drizzle in the leftover oil & continue to blend until incorporated well.
6. Add the roasted vegetables and dressing to the bowl with wild rice. Gently toss to mix the ingredients; serve and enjoy.

Three Sisters Bowl with Hominy, Beans & Squash

Prep Time: 10 minutes
Cooking Time: 50 minutes
Servings: 04

Ingredients

- 1 small, unpeeled acorn squash (approximately 1¼ pounds), halved, seeds & membranes scraped away, then cut into 1" chunks
- ½ cup dried brown tepary beans
- 1 tablespoon New Mexico Hatch Chile powder
- ½ cup dried hominy
- 2 teaspoons chopped fresh sage
- 1 small yellow onion, halved & thinly sliced
- ½ cup dark greens, chopped, such as spinach, kale, or dandelion greens
- 3 tablespoons sunflower oil
- Coarse sea salt & smoked sea salt, as needed

Directions

1. Place the tepary beans and hominy in separate medium-sized bowls. Add water to each bowl (enough to cover the beans by 4"); soak them at room temperature for overnight.
2. Just 3 hours prior to serving, drain the beans and the hominy; place them in separate 3-to-4-quart pots. Add cool water enough to cover the tepary beans and hominy by 4". Set each over high heat and bring to a boil. Once done; decrease the heat & let simmer gently for up to 2 hours, until tender, skimming any foam & stirring occasionally.
3. Reserve approximately ⅔ cup of the cooking liquid from each type of beans. Drain the beans and the hominy; set aside.
4. In the meantime, prepare the squash. Preheat your oven to 425F. Toss the squash with 1 tablespoon oil and a pinch of coarse sea salt on a rimmed baking sheet lined with parchment. Arrange the squash in an even layer & roast for 35 to 45 minutes, until very tender and golden, stirring halfway.
5. Next, over moderate heat in a large skillet; heat the leftover oil until hot. Add the onion followed by sage, chili powder and a generous pinch of smoked salt; cook for 5 to 8 minutes, until the onions are tender, stirring occasionally. Add the kept-aside cooking liquid & bring it to a simmer.
6. Add the cooked beans and hominy to the skillet; stir in the roasted greens and squash. Season with coarse sea salt to taste; serve immediately and enjoy.

Roasted Turnips

Prep Time: 20 minutes
Cooking Time: 40 minutes
Servings: 08

Ingredients

- 2 shallots, sliced
- 4 tablespoons unsalted butter, cubed
- 2 pounds turnips with purple tops, cut into wedges
- 3 sprigs fresh thyme
- 1 tablespoon olive oil
- Freshly ground black pepper & kosher salt to taste

Directions

1. Preheat your oven to 450F.
2. Toss the turnips with shallots, thyme sprigs, butter, olive oil and some of pepper and salt in a large baking dish.
3. Roast in the preheated oven for 30 minutes, until the turnips start to soften.
4. Taste and adjust the amount of seasoning to your likings; serve and enjoy.

Roasted Delicata Squash

Prep Time: 20 minutes
Cooking Time: 20 minutes
Servings: 02

Ingredients

- 1 large Delicata squash; ends trimmed, lengthwise halved & seeded
- ⅛ teaspoon cayenne pepper, or to taste
- 1 teaspoon salt
- 1 tablespoon olive oil

Directions

1. Preheat your oven to 450F.
2. Line a large-sized, rimmed baking sheet with a silicone mat or the parchment paper.
3. Place the squash halves on a large cutting board, cut side down. Cut into 3/8" slices; transfer the slices to a large bowl and then, drizzle with the olive oil; add cayenne pepper and salt. Gently toss until the squash is coated well. Arrange the squash on the prepared baking sheet in a single layer.
4. Bake for 12 to 18 minutes, until squash is tender, and the bottoms are browned. Serve and enjoy.

Roasted Butternut Squash

Prep Time: 30 minutes
Cooking Time: 30 minutes
Servings: 04

Ingredients

- 2 garlic cloves, minced
- 1 butternut squash, medium-sized
- 2 tablespoons olive oil
- Ground black pepper & salt to taste

Directions

1. Preheat the oven to 400 degrees F (200 degrees C).
2. Peel the butternut squash using a very sharp vegetable peeler and then, cut lengthwise into half; scoop out & discard the seeds. Cut the halves into 1" slices and then, cut the slices into 1" cubes.
3. Combine the butternut squash cubes with garlic, and olive oil in a large-sized mixing bowl; gently toss until coated well. Season with pepper and salt. Arrange on a baking sheet in a single layer.
4. Roast for 25 to 35 minutes, until the squash is browned lightly & tender.

Squash Stew

Prep Time: 20 minutes
Cooking Time: 1 hour & 30 minutes
Servings: 04

Ingredients

- 1 pound butternut squash, trimmed & cut into 2" cubes
- 2 garlic cloves, chopped
- 1 tablespoon fresh rosemary, minced
- 2 pounds stew beef, cut into 2" cubes
- 1 tablespoon fresh thyme, chopped
- 2 tablespoons all-purpose flour
- ¼ cup sun-dried tomatoes, chopped
- 3 to 4 cups beef broth
- 1 onion, peeled & chopped
- 2 tablespoons fresh flat-leaf parsley, chopped
- 1 cup Marsala wine
- 3 tablespoon olive oil
- ½ teaspoon each of freshly ground black pepper and salt, plus more to taste
- Crusty bread, for serving

Directions

1. Over moderate heat in a large soup pot; heat 3 tablespoons of olive oil until hot.
2. Once done; add the onions with garlic, thyme, and rosemary; sauté for 2 minutes, until the onions are tender.
3. Toss the beef cubes in pepper, flour, and salt. Increase the heat to high; add the beef to the pot & cook for 5 minutes, until the beef is golden and browned around the edges. Add in the Marsala wine.
4. Gently stir up all the brown bits off the bottom of your pan using a large wooden spoon. Add the sun-dried tomatoes & butternut squash; stir until mixed well. Add enough beef broth to just cover the squash and beef. Bring the stew to a boil over high heat.
5. Once done; decrease the heat to low; cover & let simmer for an hour. Season the stew with more of pepper and salt to taste. Sprinkle with the fresh chopped parsley.
6. Serve with the crusty bread on side and enjoy.

Savory Pumpkin

Prep Time: 20 minutes
Cooking Time: 30 minutes
Servings: 06

Ingredients

- 1 pound ground turkey or beef
- 3 cups chicken, vegetable, or beef broth
- 1 medium yellow onion, diced
- 3 medium russet potatoes, diced
- 1 can white beans (15-oz), drained & rinsed
- 4 cups curly kale, stems removed & torn into small, bite-sized pieces
- 1 ½ tablespoons olive oil
- ⅔ cup coconut milk, full fat
- 1 can pumpkin puree (15-oz)

For Spices:
- 4 bay leaves, medium
- ¼ teaspoon black pepper
- 2 tablespoons dried basil
- ½ teaspoon salt

Directions

1. Over moderate heat in a large pot; heat the olive oil and add the onion; sauté for 5 minutes, until the onions begin to caramelize and are soft, stirring occasionally.
2. Add ground meat to the pot & cook for 5 to 7 minutes, until browned, stirring occasionally.
3. Add all the other ingredients to your pot (except coconut milk & kale). Give the ingredients a good stir. Heat to a simmer & cook for 15 minutes, until the potatoes are soft, stirring occasionally.
4. Lastly add the kale followed by ⅔ cup of coconut milk. Bring the mix to a simmer! Serve warm & enjoy.

Comanche-style Corn

Prep Time: 20 minutes
Cooking Time: 20 minutes
Servings: 02

Ingredients

- 1 bell pepper, diced
- 4 ounces bacon (cooked & diced)
- 1 can chilies (4 ounce)
- 2 cups whole kernel corn, frozen
- 1 yellow onion, diced
- A pinch each of black pepper & salt
- 1 garlic clove, crushed

Directions

1. Fry the bacon until done. Let it cool and then, tear into small pieces.
2. Leave the bacon grease inside the pot & set aside.
3. Next, sauté the onion in the kept-aside grease until clear. Add the bacon, garlic, corn, chilies, pepper & salt. Let simmer over a low heat until heated through, stirring often.
4. Once done, drain the grease; serve and enjoy.

Fried Green Tomatoes

Prep Time: 10 minutes
Cooking Time: 20 minutes
Servings: 04

Ingredients

- 4 green tomatoes, large; sliced into ½" thick & discard the ends
- ½ cup cornmeal
- 1 cup all-purpose flour
- ½ cup breadcrumbs
- 2 large eggs
- ½ cup milk
- 2 teaspoons coarse kosher salt
- 1 quart vegetable oil, as required, for frying
- ¼ teaspoon ground black pepper

Directions

1. Whisk the eggs with milk in a medium-sized mixing bowl until mixed well. Scoop the flour onto a large plate. Combine the cornmeal with breadcrumbs, pepper, and salt on a separate plate. Dip the tomatoes into flour and ensure that the pieces are nicely coated and then dip into the egg-milk mixture. Dredge into the breadcrumbs and ensure that the pieces are completely coated.
2. Next, fill a large skillet with approximately ½" of vegetable oil & place it over moderate heat.
3. Work in batches; place the coated tomatoes carefully into the frying pan; ensure that you don't crowd the tomatoes.
4. Cook until the tomatoes turn brown; flip & fry other side until turn brown as well. Place them on paper towels to drain.

Roasted Turnips & Winter Squash with Agave Glaze

Prep Time: 20 minutes
Cooking Time: 50 minutes
Servings: 10

Ingredients

- 2 delicata squash or 1 small butternut squash (2 pounds in total), unpeeled, halved, seeds & membranes scraped away; cut into 1" chunks
- 2 pounds turnips, trimmed and cut into 1" chunks
- 2 tablespoons light agave nectar
- 2 tablespoons fresh sage, chopped
- ¼ cup sunflower seeds, toasted
- 2 tablespoons sunflower oil
- 2 teaspoons coarse sea salt

Directions

1. Line 2 large-sized roasting pans or baking sheets with foil or parchment and then, preheat your oven to 425F.
2. Next, toss the turnips with squash, oil, salt, and sage in a large-sized mixing bowl. Evenly divide the mixture between the baking sheets and then, spread in an even layer.
3. Transfer to your preheated oven; roast for 20 minutes on the lower and middle shelves, stirring the vegetables & rotating the baking sheets halfway. Decrease the heat to 400 F & continue roasting for 10 to 20 minutes more, until tender and caramelized, stirring & rotating halfway again.
4. Remove from the oven & brush with the agave. Continue cooking for 2 to 3 minutes, until the vegetables appear glossy. Serve with sunflower seeds scattered on top. Enjoy.

Tepary Beans with Chile-Agave Glaze

Prep Time: 40 minutes
Cooking Time: 2 hours & 20 minutes
Servings: 08

Ingredients

- 1 cup white tepary beans, dried
- ½ small yellow onion, thinly sliced
- 1 tablespoon chipotle powder or Chile powder, plus additional for garnish
- 3 tablespoons light agave nectar
- 1 cup brown tepary beans, dried
- 2 teaspoons whole fresh oregano leaves
- 1 tablespoon sunflower oil
- Sea salt

Directions

1. Place the brown and white tepary beans in a large-sized bowl. Add water enough to cover by 4"; let them soak at room temperature for overnight.
2. Drain the soaked beans, discarding the liquid & transfer the beans to a large pot with a tight-fitting lid. Add enough of cool water to cover the beans by approximately 4". Bring it to a boil over high heat.
3. Once done; decrease the heat; cover & let gently simmer for 2 hours, until the beans are tender, stirring occasionally. Reserve approximately 1 cup of the bean cooking liquid then drain the beans.
4. Next, over moderate heat in a large, deep skillet; heat the oil until hot. Add and sauté the onion for 3 minutes, until translucent. Add the cooked beans & kept-aside bean cooking liquid followed by the Chile powder and the agave. Cook for 10 minutes, until the liquid has decreased to a glaze, stirring occasionally. Season with salt to taste. Evenly divide among the bowls and then, sprinkle with more of Chile powder & top with the oregano. Enjoy

Main Dishes

Tamales

Prep Time: 30 minutes
Cooking Time: 3 hours & 20 minutes
Servings: 16

Ingredients

For Husks and Dough:
- 1 can beef broth (10.5 ounce), or as required
- ⅔ cup lard
- 1 package dried corn husks (8 ounce)
- 2 cups masa harina
- 1 cup sour cream
- ½ teaspoon salt
- 1 teaspoon baking powder

For Filling:
- 1 large onion, halved
- 1 ¼ pounds pork loin
- 1 garlic clove

For Chile Sauce:
- 4 Chile peppers, dried
- 1 ½ teaspoons salt
- 2 cups water

Directions

1. For Filling: Place the pork with garlic, and onion in a large Dutch oven. Add water (enough to cover); bring it to a boil, over moderate heat. Decrease the heat to low & let simmer for 2 hours, until pork is cooked through.
2. In the meantime, prepare the Chile sauce. Remove the seeds & stems from chilies using rubber gloves. Place the chilies with 2 cups of water in a large saucepan. Let simmer for 20 minutes, uncovered. Remove from the heat & let cool.
3. Transfer the chilies & cooking water to a blender, blend on high power until completely smooth. Strain the mixture into a large bowl & stir in the salt; set the mix aside.
4. Shred the cooked pork & mix in 1 cup of the Chile sauce. Reserve the leftover sauce for serving.
5. For Husks & Dough: Soak the corn husks in a bowl of warm water for 30 minutes, until softened.
6. Meanwhile, beat the lard with 1 tablespoon of broth until completely fluffy. Combine the masa harina with salt, and baking powder in a separate bowl; stir into the prepared lard mixture, adding more of broth as required to get spongy dough like consistency.
7. Remove the husks from water & pat dry. Spread the dough out over the husks to ¼ to ½" thick.
8. Place 1 tablespoon of the pork filling in middle of each. Fold the sides, bottom, and top of each husk in toward the middle to enclose the dough.
9. Arrange the tamales in a steamer basket. Place on top of the simmering water & steam for an hour.
10. Remove the tamales from husks. Drizzle with the leftover Chile sauce & top with sour cream.

Pemmican

Prep Time: 20 minutes
Cooking Time: 20 minutes
Servings: 16

Ingredients

- 400 grams melted beef tallow
- 100 grams ground beef liver, dry
- 2 tablespoons herbs & spices, optional
- 300 grams ground lean meat, dry
- 1 tablespoon salt

Directions

1. Mix the dry meat, liver & salt in a medium-sized mixing bowl. Add the herbs & spices; continue to mix the ingredients until mixed well.
2. Heat the tallow over moderate heat in a double boiler until melted.
3. Pour on top of the dry ingredients; thoroughly stir until mixed well. Break all clumps apart. If the meat appears to be still crumbly, feel free to add more of melted fat.
4. Evenly spread the prepared mixture into a large baking dish; set aside at room temperature to harden. Once firm, score into desired squares.

Duck & Wild Rice Pemmican

Prep Time: 20 minutes
Cooking Time: 50 minutes
Servings: 04

Ingredients

- 4 tablespoons maple sugar
- 2 duck breasts with skin
- ¼ cup wild rice, raw
- 4 ounces dried blueberries
- 1 tablespoon salt

Directions

1. Remove the duck fat from breasts & place over low heat in a shallow sauté pan for 45 minutes, to render the fat; remove the fat & reserve the oil.

Dry Duck:
1. Mix maple sugar and salt
2. Slice the duck breast along the grain into thin, long strips
3. Rub the duck breast strips with the prepared sugar-salt mix
4. Dehydrate the duck strips either in a food dehydrator or in oven at very low heat until dry

Pop Wild Rice:
1. Heat duck fat on low heat in a sauté pan & place wild rice in the pan
2. Stir & shake the pan until the wild rice starts to "pop" & "puff"
3. Remove the wild rice & place on paper towel

Mix all the ingredients & form into small bites:
1. Place all the ingredients (crisp duck fat, puffed wild rice, dried duck, dried blueberries, and any leftover duck fat oil) in a food processor
2. Mix until consistent then, form into small bites & garnish with more of puffed wild rice. Serve immediately & enjoy.

Wild Turkey Green Chili Tamale Pie

Prep Time: 20 minutes
Cooking Time: 10 minutes
Servings: 16

Ingredients

For Masa & Corn Husks
- 1 bag dried corn husks (8-ounce)
- 5 ounces chilled lard (⅔ cup)
- 1 teaspoon baking powder
- 2 cups dried masa mix for tamales (don't use masa harina)
- 1 cup cool chicken or turkey broth
- Salt

For Filling
- 2 cups cooked turkey, shredded (½ pound)
- ½ pound fresh tomatillos, husked
- 2 tablespoons white onion, chopped & soaked for 5 minutes in cold water, drained & rinsed
- 1 cup chicken or turkey broth
- 6 to 12 cilantro sprigs, plus chopped cilantro for garnish
- 1 large garlic clove, peeled
- ½ teaspoon chipotle powder or crushed dried chipotle chiles
- 1 tablespoon grapeseed or canola oil
- 2 serrano chiles or jalapeño, stemmed
- Salt to taste

Directions

1. For Corn Husks: Fill a large saucepan with water & bring it to a boil, over moderate heat. Turn the heat off & submerge the husks using a plate; let soak for an hour.
2. In the meantime, prepare the masa: Mix the masa with 1¼ cups of hot water in a medium-sized mixing bowl; let cool.
3. Combine the lard with baking powder in a stand mixer; beat until light, for a minute. Add masa and salt in 3 additions, beating at medium-low speed. Slowly add ¾ cup of broth while beating on low speed; beat for a minute or two. Taste for salt. Test to see if masa is aerated enough by dropping ½ teaspoon into a cup of water; it should

float to the top. Cover & refrigerate for an hour. Beat the masa again for a few minutes, adding the leftover broth.

4. In the meantime, prepare the filling. Place the tomatillos in a saucepan. Add water (enough to cover) & bring it to a boil, over moderate heat. Once done; decrease the heat & let simmer until softened and olive green, for 8 to 10 minutes, flipping halfway. Drain & place in a blender. Add the green chiles followed by onion, cilantro, and garlic. Blend on high power until completely smooth.

5. Next, over moderate heat in a large, heavy skillet or saucepan; heat the oil until hot. Add the tomatillo purée; continue to stir until it thickens and starts to stick to the pan, for a couple of minutes. Stir in the broth, add salt to taste & bring it to a simmer. Let simmer for 10 to 12 minutes, stirring now and then. Stir in the chipotles. Taste & adjust the amount of seasoning. Remove from heat and immediately stir in the shredded turkey.

6. For Tamales: Select 16 corn husks; look for large ones that have no tears. Take a few more and tear into 16¼" wide strips for tying tamales. Use some of the leftover husks to line a steamer that is at least 6" deep; reserve a few husks in case you need to double-wrap tamales. Add just enough water to the pot to miss hitting the bottom of the basket.

7. Lay a corn husk in front of you and pat dry. Spread a scant ¼ cup of the masa into a 4-inch square, leaving a 1½" border at pointy tapered end of the husk and a roughly ¾" border on the other sides. Spoon a heaped tablespoon of turkey mixture down the middle of the masa. Pull long edges of husk toward each other and join them so that batter is now wrapped around the filling. Fold the two pinched-together edges over in the same direction and wrap the tamale. If it does not seem well wrapped, wrap in a second husk. Fold pointy end up to enclose the bottom and tie with a strip of husk. The wide top end will be open. Stand tamale up, closed end down, in steamer. Repeat with remaining masa and filling. The tamales should be crowded into the steamer, so they remain upright. If they don't, fill spaces with crinkled foil. If tops stick out from top of steamer, trim with scissors.

8. Lay soaked husks over tops of tamales. Bring water to a boil, cover pot, reduce heat to medium and steam tamales for 1½ hours. Meanwhile, bring a kettle of water to a boil to replenish water in bottom of the pot, should it run out (check periodically). Tamales are done when husk comes away easily from the masa; when done, let them sit at least 15 minutes in the pot, uncovered, to firm up. Serve hot.

Poyha Chicken & Cornbread Loaf

Prep Time: 10 minutes
Cooking Time: 1 hour & 20 minutes
Servings: 08

Ingredients

- 3 slices bacon, chopped
- 1 large yellow onion, diced
- 2 cups green seedless grapes, chopped fine
- 1 ¼ cups coarse yellow cornmeal
- 2 pounds ground chicken or ground turkey
- ½ teaspoon pepper
- 3 large eggs
- Pam cooking spray
- 2 cans whole kernel corn (14 ounce each), drained
- ½ teaspoon garlic salt
- 3 tablespoons oil
- Paprika, to taste

Directions

1. Chop the corn in a food chopper or blender until very small pieces; set aside.
2. Next, add the chopped corn with chopped onion, grapes, pepper, and eggs in a large-sized mixing bowl. Beat until the eggs are mixed; set aside. Feel free to add the garlic salt and paprika to the mixing bowl.

Dutch Oven or Cast-Iron Skillet:

1. Brown the ground meat in the raw chopped bacon pieces or in the oil. Cook until just brown; ensure that you don't overcook. Add the drained meat to the corn mixture. Wipe the Dutch oven or skillet clean using a paper towel. Season with a bit of oil or grease.
2. Add cornmeal to the meat-corn mixture; mix well using your hands. Slowly add more of cornmeal if the mixture appears to be runny.
3. Pack into cast iron Dutch oven. Cover.
4. Put on the grill for 45 minutes to 1 hour, on moderate heat. Over hot coals for 45 minutes. Let cool for 15 minutes. Cut the slices in the Dutch oven and then, lift the slices out to the serving dish.

For Meat Loaf Pans:

1. Spray with Pam and pack into two loaf pans.
2. Bake for 45 minutes at 350 F.
3. Serve with white sauce, gravy, ketchup.

Sumac Chicken with Onions

Prep Time: 20 minutes
Cooking Time: 50 minutes
Servings: 04

Ingredients

- 2 pounds skin-on, bone-in chicken thighs & drumsticks
- Juice of 1 large lemon, fresh
- 4 garlic cloves, crushed
- 1½ tablespoons sumac, plus additional for serving
- ½ teaspoon ground allspice
- 1 large red onion, halved & thinly sliced
- ¼ teaspoon ground cinnamon
- 2 tablespoons pine nuts
- ½ teaspoon ground cumin
- 4 tablespoons extra-virgin olive oil, plus additional for serving
- Ground black pepper & sea salt to taste

For Serving:
- Arabic taboon bread or Naan
- Fresh parsley leaves, coarsely chopped

Directions

1. Slash the flesh of chicken pieces diagonally a couple of times, around ¾" apart and then, place the meat in a large plastic container or bowl. Add the lemon juice followed by 3 tablespoons olive oil, the garlic, 1½ tablespoons sumac, cumin, cinnamon, and allspice; and ¼ teaspoon pepper and 1½ teaspoons salt. Rub the prepared mixture into the meat. Add the red onion; gently toss to coat. Cover & transfer to the refrigerator; let marinate for a couple of hours.
2. Once ready, preheat your oven to 375 F. Transfer the meat with onion slices & any accumulated juices to the baking sheet & roast for 40 minutes. Once done, tightly cover the baking sheet with the aluminum foil; set aside while you prepare the toppings.
3. Cook the pine nuts in the leftover olive oil over low heat in a small skillet for 2 minutes, until turn golden brown, stirring now and then. Transfer to a paper towel to drain.
4. To serve, heat the taboon bread or naan in the oven until warmed & toasted, transfer to a large platter. Arrange the chicken & red onion on top. Finish with a smattering of sumac, pine nuts & chopped parsley. Drizzle any leftover roasting juices and with a bit more of olive oil.

Colorado Buffalo Chili

Prep Time: 50 minutes
Cooking Time: 8 hours & 30 minutes
Servings: 06

Ingredients

- 1 pound ground buffalo
- ½ teaspoon ground cumin
- 1 can kidney beans (14.5 ounce), drained
- ½ medium onion, chopped
- 1 can chili beans (15 ounce), drained
- ½ teaspoon minced garlic
- 1 poblano chili pepper, chopped
- 2 tablespoons chili powder
- 1 can tomato soup (10.75 ounce)
- 1 ½ teaspoons ground cumin
- 1 teaspoon red pepper flakes
- ½ teaspoon cayenne pepper
- 1 can diced tomatoes with green chiles (10 ounce)
- A pinch cayenne pepper, or to taste
- 1 Anaheim Chile pepper, chopped
- Ground black pepper & salt to taste

Directions

1. Over moderate heat in a large skillet; brown the buffalo and then, season with approximately a pinch of cayenne pepper and ½ teaspoon of cumin, or to taste. Drain any additional grease.
2. Next, mix the buffalo with tomato soup, tomatoes with green chiles, chili beans, kidney beans, onion, garlic, poblano chili pepper, Anaheim chili pepper, red pepper flakes, 1 ½ teaspoons cumin, ½ teaspoon cayenne pepper, chili powder, black pepper, and salt in a slow cooker. Cover & cook for 8 hours on Low heat.

Harvest Chicken Casserole

Prep Time: 20 minutes
Cooking Time: 60 minutes
Servings: 08

Ingredients

- ½ cup almonds, sliced
- 2 pounds boneless skinless chicken breasts
- ½ onion, chopped
- 2 medium sweet potatoes, peeled and cut into small cubes
- 1 pounds Brussels sprouts, trimmed & quartered
- 6 cups wild rice, cooked
- ½ cup dried cranberries
- 2 garlic cloves, minced
- ½ cup chicken broth, low sodium, divided
- 2 teaspoons fresh thyme leaves
- 1 teaspoon paprika
- ½ teaspoon ground cumin
- 2 tablespoons extra-virgin olive oil, divided, plus more for baking dish
- Freshly ground black pepper & kosher salt to taste

Directions

1. Grease a large baking dish with oil and then, preheat your oven to 350F.
2. Next, over moderate heat in a large, deep skillet; heat 1 tablespoon of oil until hot. Season the chicken with pepper and salt. Add to the hot skillet & cook for 8 minutes on each side, until cooked through and golden. Let rest for a couple of minutes and then, cut into 1" pieces.
3. Heat one more tablespoon of oil over moderate heat. Add onion, garlic, Brussels sprouts, sweet potatoes, thyme, cumin, and paprika. Season with pepper and salt; cook for 5 minutes, until softened. Add ¼ cup of broth; bring it to a simmer & cook for 5 minutes, covered.
4. Place the cooked rice in a large baking dish & season with pepper and salt. Stir in the chicken, cooked vegetables, cranberries, and leftover broth. Top with almonds & bake for 15 to 18 more minutes, until almonds are toasted, and dish is hot. Enjoy.

Bison Meatballs with Wild Rice

Prep Time: 30 minutes
Cooking Time: 30 minutes
Servings: 20

Ingredients

- 2 pounds ground bison
- ½ cup red onion, diced
- 2 tablespoons duck fat
- 1 cup cooked wild rice, cooled
- 2 tablespoons tomato paste
- ½ cup cranberries, dried
- 1 tablespoon Montreal steak seasoning

Optional Ingredients:
- Chopped fresh herbs
- Kosher salt

Directions

1. Line a medium-sized baking sheet with the aluminum foil and then, preheat your oven to 350F.
2. Next, over moderate heat in a medium skillet, heat the fat. Cook the onions for 4 to 6 minutes, until translucent.
3. Add tomato paste to the onions & cook for 10 more minutes, until darkened. Remove from the heat.
4. Stir the wild rice with dried cranberries, onion-tomato paste mixture, and steak seasoning to combine in a large bowl.
5. Add bison; give it a good stir until incorporated well. Feel free to season your recipe with the kosher salt, if needed.
6. Portion the meat into 20 meatballs using a heaping 1 ½ tablespoon cookie scoop. Transfer to the prepared baking sheet & bake for 15 to 20 minutes. Serve hot and enjoy.

Bison Pot Roast with Hominy

Prep Time: 30 minutes
Cooking Time: 3 hours & 50 minutes
Servings: 08

Ingredients

- 1 bison chuck roast (approximately 3 to 4 pounds)
- 3 to 4 cups vegetable or bison stock
- 1 packed cup dandelion greens, sliced
- 2 fresh sage sprigs, plus additional leaves kept-aside for garnish
- 1 branch wild white cedar (approximately 4"), or 2 teaspoons dried juniper berries
- ¼ cup light agave nectar
- 1 cup dried hominy
- 3 tablespoons sunflower oil
- Coarse sea salt

Directions

1. Add hominy to a large-sized mixing bowl and add water (enough to cover the same by 3"). Let soak at room temperature for overnight. Drain & discard the soaking liquid.
2. Next, preheat your oven to 250F. Generously season the bison with 2 tablespoons of salt on all sides.
3. Over moderate heat in a large, heavy pot or Dutch oven; heat the oil until hot. Add the bison & sear until browned on all sides, rotating the meat halfway. Transfer the meat to a large plate and then, add the drained hominy followed by cedar, sage sprigs, stock, and agave to the pot.
4. Bring the mix to a simmer, scraping down the sides and bottom of your pot. Add meat back to the pot, cover & transfer to the oven. Bake for 3 to 3½ hours, until the meat is very tender, turning halfway.
5. Remove & discard the cedar and sage sprigs. Stir in the greens until wilted. Season the liquid with additional salt to taste.
6. Slice the meat into 1" thick slabs & evenly divide among the shallow bowls. Spoon some of the sauce, greens, and hominy on top of the slices & garnish with torn or whole sage leaves.

Crawfish & Shrimp Pot with Spiced Sweet Potatoes

Prep Time: 50 minutes
Cooking Time: 1 hour & 20 minutes
Servings: 04

Ingredients

- 1 pound jumbo shrimp, head-on
- 2 pounds crawfish
- 1 tablespoon red-pepper flakes, plus additional as required
- ½ packed cup sliced dandelion greens, plus whole leaves for garnish
- 1 tablespoon coarse sea salt, plus more as needed
- 2 tablespoons New Mexico red Chile powder or chipotle Chile powder
- 1 small purple or orange sweet potato, unpeeled, cut into ½" cubes
- 2 tablespoons sunflower oil
- 1 cup yellow onion, chopped
- ½ cup fresh blackberries
- 1 tablespoon filé powder

Directions

1. Fill a large pot with the red-pepper flakes, 3 quarts of water and salt. Bring it to a boil, over moderate heat. Once done; immediately add the shrimp and crawfish, bring it to a boil again. Decrease the heat & let simmer for 10 minutes, until the shellfish turns deep red; skimming any foam off that rises to the surface. Turn the heat off; cover & let stand for a couple of minutes.

2. In the meantime, prepare the vegetables. Over moderate heat in a large skillet, heat the oil until hot. Add and sauté the onion for 3 minutes, until it starts to soften. Add the sweet potato, filé powder, 2 cups of the shellfish cooking water and Chile powder; bring the mix to a boil, over moderate heat. Once done; decrease the heat to medium & let simmer until the sweet potatoes turn tender, for 8 to 10 minutes, stirring occasionally.

3. Stir in the sliced greens and blackberries; continue to cook for a minute or two. Gently mash the blackberries using the tip of a wooden spoon or the back of a fork & season the mix with red-pepper flakes and coarse sea salt to taste.

4. Spoon the vegetables onto a large platter or individual plates. Strain the shrimp and crawfish mixture then, arrange the cooked shellfish over the vegetables. Garnish with the kept-aside leaves. Enjoy.

Roasted Trout

Prep Time: 40 minutes
Cooking Time: 40 minutes
Servings: 12

Ingredients

- 1 whole trout (1.5kg), scaled & pin-boned, from sustainable sources
- 4 large tomatoes, ripe
- 1 lemon
- Olive oil, as needed
- 1 onion
- 50 g softened unsalted butter, at room temperature
- A bunch each of fresh dill, and fresh parsley

Directions

1. Preheat your oven to 350F.
2. Peel the onion & finely slice with the lemon and tomatoes. Roughly chop the parsley and dill (stalks and all). Coat a large baking tray lightly with a bit of oil, scatter over ⅓ of the sliced tomato, lemon & herbs; top with the fish and season the skin and cavity with black pepper and sea salt.
3. Stuff the cavity with one more third of the sliced tomato, lemon, and herbs; scatter the leftover third on top. Don't forget to arrange some of the tomatoes around the fish. Dot with the butter and then, drizzle with 2 tablespoons of oil on all sides then, a twist of black pepper.
4. Roast until just cooked through, for 25 minutes. Enjoy.

Pine Nut Catfish

Prep Time: 20 minutes
Cooking Time: 20 minutes
Servings: 04

Ingredients

- 4 catfish fillets
- ¼ cup flour
- 2 tablespoons pine nuts
- ¼ teaspoon ground cumin
- ½ cup yellow cornmeal
- ¼ cup pine nuts, plus
- 1 teaspoon salt
- ½ teaspoon cayenne pepper
- ¼ cup vegetable oil

Directions

1. Preheat your oven to 350F.
2. Spread the pine nuts on a large-sized baking sheet & toast in the preheated oven until turn golden brown, for 5 minutes. Let cool.
3. Grind ¼ cup of the pine nuts & reserve the leftover nuts for garnish.
4. Next, combine the ground pine nuts with flour, cornmeal, cumin, cayenne pepper and salt in a large shallow dish until mixed well.
5. Dredge the fillets into the pine nut mix & set aside.
6. Next, over moderate heat in a large skillet; heat the oil until hot. Carefully fry the catfish fillets (in batches) until fish flakes easily, for 4 minutes per side.
7. Sprinkle the fillets with whole pine nuts; serve immediately and enjoy.

Bone-in Bison Steaks

Prep Time: 20 minutes
Cooking Time: 30 minutes
Servings: 12

Ingredients

- 2 ½ pounds fingerling potatoes
- ¼ cup fresh parsley, chopped
- 12 thick-cut, bone-in bison or beef tenderloin steaks
- Freshly ground pepper & kosher salt to taste
- 2 tablespoons Apple-Cider Vinegar
- 1 cup olive oil
- Nasturtium Chimichurri Sauce, as needed

For Nasturtium Chimichurri Sauce
- 2 garlic cloves
- 1 cup arugula or nasturtium leaves
- 1 ½ cups Italian parsley
- ½ cup fresh mint leaves
- 3 tablespoons white wine vinegar
- 1 teaspoon capers
- 3 tablespoons lemon juice
- ½ cup extra-virgin olive oil

Directions

1 Preheat your grill over moderate heat in advance. Rub the steaks with olive oil and then, pepper and salt to taste; transfer to a large-sized baking sheet; set aside.

2 Next, over moderate heat in a large cast-iron skillet; heat the oil until hot. Add boiled potatoes to the hot skillet & cook for 6 to 8 minutes, until crispy and golden brown, flipping halfway.

3 Remove from the heat; add cider vinegar and pepper and salt to taste. Sprinkle with parsley; give it a good stir to combine. Let the potatoes to rest in the pan while you cook the steaks.

4 In the meantime, grill the steaks for 8 minutes on each side, until meat is medium-rare and grill marks develop, flipping halfway. Arrange the potatoes on a large serving platter, top with the steaks. Place a heaping tablespoon of chimichurri sauce on every steak & sprinkle with the salt; serve immediately.

For Chimichurri Sauce:

1. Add 1 ½ cups of Italian parsley with arugula or nasturtium leaves, garlic cloves, mint leaves, capers, and pepper and salt to taste in bowl of a food processor; pulse on high power until herbs are finely chopped.

2. With the food processor still running on low speed, slowly pour in extra-virgin olive oil followed by lemon juice and white wine vinegar. Add more of pepper & salt to taste; stir until mixed well.

Pueblo Pork Roast

Prep Time: 20 minutes
Cooking Time: 4 hours & 20 minutes
Servings: 06

Ingredients

- 5 pounds pork rib roast
- 1 ½ cups onions, chopped
- 4 dried juniper berries, crushed
- ½ teaspoon coriander seed, crushed
- 4 large ripe tomatoes, quartered & seeded
- 1 bay leaf
- 3 garlic cloves, minced
- 1 tablespoon ground New Mexico red chili
- 2/3 cup cider vinegar
- 1 medium-hot dried New Mexico Chile, crushed
- ½ cup honey
- 1-ounce unsweetened chocolate square, grated
- 2 teaspoons salt
- ¼ cup vegetable oil
- 1 ¼ cups water

Directions

1. Over moderate heat in a large, heavy saucepan; heat the oil until hot and sauté the onions until soft.
2. Once done; add the garlic followed by juniper berries, bay leaf, and coriander seed; continue to sauté for 2 to 3 more minutes.
3. Add tomatoes followed by vinegar, water, ground and crushed chili, honey, and salt.
4. Cover & let simmer for 30 minutes.
5. Add the chocolate & let simmer until thick, for 20 to 30 minutes, uncovered.
6. Preheat your oven to 350F.
7. Place the roast in a roasting pan, fat side up and generously baste with the prepared sauce.
8. Roast for 3 hours, basting occasionally with the prepared sauce & pan drippings.
9. Let the roast to sit for a couple of minutes in a warm place before carving.
10. Slice & spoon more of sauce on top of each portion. Enjoy.

Roast Turkey with Berry-Mint Sauce & Black Walnuts

Prep Time: 30 minutes
Cooking Time: 40 minutes
Servings: 08

Ingredients

- 3 cups wild rice cooking liquid or turkey stock, plus additional as needed
- 1 heritage breed turkey (10 to 12 pounds)
- 3 cups blackberries or raspberries, fresh
- A bunch of fresh sage
- 6 medium leeks (pale green and white portions only), halved lengthwise then, cut into 2" pieces & rinsed clean
- ½ cup black walnuts, lightly toasted & chopped
- 2 tablespoons sunflower oil
- Coarse sea salt
- 2 tablespoons fresh mint, chopped, plus additional as needed
- ½ cup maple syrup, plus additional as needed
- 3 cups cranberries, fresh or frozen
- Pea shoots or microgreens, for garnish

Directions

1. Remove the giblets from the cavity; discard or keep it aside for another use. Pat dries the turkey using paper towels. Once done; rub the turkey with approximately ½ teaspoon salt per pound of turkey on all sides. Tuck the sage sprigs inside the turkey cavity.
2. Set the turkey, breast-side up on a large baking sheet. Place in the refrigerator for 4 to 6 hours, uncovered to dry out the skin.
3. Once done, remove the turkey from refrigerator & let it come to room temperature.
4. Preheat your oven to 450F. Pour the stock or rice cooking liquid into a large roasting pan & add the leeks. Place a roasting rack on top and then, transfer the turkey, breast-side up to the roasting rack; tuck the wings underneath. Generously brush the exposed turkey with the oil. Transfer to the preheated oven & roast for 30 minutes; basting the turkey with the pan juices. Feel free to add more of stock or rice cooking liquid as required and ensure that there is a ½" layer of liquid at the bottom of your pan.
5. Decrease your oven's temperature to 350 F & continue to roast for 1 to 1½ hours, basting after every 30 minutes. Brush with ¼ cup of maple syrup over the turkey. Transfer the turkey to a large cutting board & let rest for half an hour before carving.
6. Transfer ¾ cup of turkey pan juices to a heavy-bottomed saucepan. Add the blackberries or raspberries, the mint, and cranberries to the saucepan, give it a good stir using a wooden spoon to combine, and bring it to a boil. Decrease the heat to medium & cook for 10 to 12 minutes, stirring occasionally. Stir in the leftover maple syrup and mint to taste.
7. Carve the turkey. Smear some of the berry sauce on each plate. Top with the leeks then the turkey. Garnish with walnuts and microgreens or pea shoots; pass more of berry sauce alongside. Enjoy.

Desserts

Appone Maize Cake

Prep Time: 20 minutes
Cooking Time: 30 minutes
Servings: 06

Ingredients

- 2 cups cornmeal
- 1 ½ cups boiling water
- 2 tablespoons margarine or melted butter
- ½ teaspoon salt

Directions

1. Preheat your oven to 375F.
2. Combine the cornmeal with butter, and salt until mixed well. Add in the boiling water (enough to make a semi-stiff mush).
3. Spread the prepared mixture approximately ½" thick in a well-greased heavy pan
4. Bake until baked through, for 20 to 25 minutes. Let cool & enjoy.

Saututhig Pudding

Prep Time: 20 minutes
Cooking Time: 1 hour & 10 minutes
Servings: 06

Ingredients

For Pudding:
- ⅓ cup milk
- 1 tablespoon apricot jam
- 6 ½ ounces sugar
- 1 teaspoon baking soda
- 2 large eggs
- 1 teaspoon vinegar
- 5 ounces all-purpose flour
- 1 tablespoon butter
- ½ teaspoon salt

For Sauce:
- 3 to 5 ounces sugar
- ¾ cup fresh cream
- 2 teaspoons vanilla essence
- 1/3 cup hot water
- 3 ½ ounces butter

Directions

1. Grease an oven dish and then, preheat your oven to 350F.
2. Whip or beat the sugar with eggs until thick & lemon colored and then, immediately add the jam (jelly) & mix through.
3. Melt the butter & add the butter with vinegar to the wet mixture.
4. Mix the flour with soda and salt. Add this mix with the milk to the egg mixture into the mixing bowl or processor. Beat well.
5. Pour into an oven-proof dish & bake for 30 to 45 minutes, until pudding is brown and well-risen.
6. Melt the ingredients together for the sauce in a pot; stir well.
7. Pour it on top of the pudding. Leave to stand for a while before serving. Serve warm.

Berry Pudding

Prep Time: 20 minutes
Cooking Time: 50 minutes
Servings: 08

Ingredients

- 125 g softened butter
- 1 cup self-rising flour
- ½ cup sugar
- 2 eggs, free-range
- 1 cup mixed berries, frozen
- ¾ cup milk
- Double cream, to serve

Directions

1. Preheat your oven to 350F.
2. Combine the butter with sugar, eggs, and flour in a large-sized mixing bowl; mix using an electric mixer for 2 minutes, on high speed.
3. Stir in the milk. Coat the baking tray or shallow pie dish lightly with the canola oil. Pour in the prepared batter & top with the fruit.
4. Bake in the preheated oven for 40 to 45 minutes. Serve warm with cold double cream and enjoy.

Sweet Cornmeal Pudding

Prep Time: 20 minutes
Cooking Time: 50 minutes
Servings: 06

Ingredients

- ¾ cup sugar
- 3 cups whole milk
- ¾ cup buttermilk
- 1 cup yellow cornmeal
- ¼ cup butter, cut into pieces
- 6 large eggs, separated
- ½ teaspoon vanilla extract
- Powdered sugar
- ½ teaspoon salt

Directions

1. Preheat your oven to 375F.
2. Butter 8 cup souffle dish. Bring milk to a boil over moderate heat in a large, heavy saucepan. Once done; decrease the heat to medium and slowly mix in the cornmeal & salt. Give it a good stir until the mixture becomes very thick.
3. Add butter; give it a good stir until completely melted. Remove the pan from heat & immediately stir in ½ cup of sugar & buttermilk. Whisk the yolks in large bowl to blend. Slowly whisk in the cornmeal mixture. Beat the egg whites in a medium-sized mixing bowl using electric mixer until completely frothy. Add the leftover sugar & continue to beat until soft peaks form. Gently fold the whites into the cornmeal mixture.
4. Transfer the mixture to the prepared dish. Bake until mixture puffs & turns golden brown. Sprinkle with the powdered sugar; serve hot and enjoy.

Wild Rice Pudding

Prep Time: 30 minutes
Cooking Time: 1 hour & 20 minutes
Servings: 06

Ingredients

- ½ cup wild rice
- ¼ cup chia seeds
- 2 ½ cups water, plus additional for soaking rice
- ¼ cup plus 1 tablespoon maple syrup, divided, plus additional for serving
- Kosher salt

For Serving:
- Sunflower seeds
- Fresh berries

Directions

1. Add wild rice to a medium saucepan & add cold water (enough to cover). Let soak for 15 minutes, uncovered.
2. Transfer the rice to a strainer & rinse a couple of times, until water runs clear.
3. Add 2 cups of water & a pinch of salt to saucepan and place it over moderate heat. Bring it to a boil.
4. Add rice; cover & cook until the rice opens, for 25 to 30 minutes, on low. Feel free to add more of water, if needed & set aside for 10 to 15 minutes to cool before blending.
5. In the meantime, bloom the chia. Combine the chia seeds with ½ cup of water & 1 tablespoon of maple syrup in a medium-sized mixing bowl.
6. Stir to combine & let sit for 5 to 10 minutes, until jelled.
7. Once the rice has cooled, immediately transfer them to the food processor with ¼ cup of maple syrup, pulse until blended well.
8. Add the Chia mixture & continue to blend until just combined and then, transfer to the refrigerator for half an hour.
9. Toast the sunflower seeds & gently toss with the berries, along with additional maple syrup.
10. Serve the pudding topped with berries and seeds. Enjoy.

Chia Pudding with Berries & Amaranth

Prep Time: 20 minutes
Cooking Time: 30 minutes
Servings: 04

Ingredients

- ¼ cup light agave nectar
- 1½ cups almond milk, unsweetened, plus additional, if required
- ½ cup chia seeds
- 1 to 2 cups fresh mixed berries
- ¼ cup amaranth
- Small fresh mint sprigs, for garnish
- ¼ cup manzanita berries, crushed, optional
- A pinch of fine sea salt

Directions

1. Whisk 1½ cups of almond milk vigorously with the agave, chia seeds and salt in a lidded quart container.
2. Let the mixture soak for 1 hour in the refrigerator. Feel free to whisk in more of almond milk, if the mixture appears to be too thick.
3. Meanwhile, over moderate heat in a small skillet; add & cook the amaranth for a minute or two, until the amaranth begins to smell toasty and about half of the seeds have popped, shaking the skillet. Transfer the amaranth to a large plate to cool to room temperature.
4. To serve, whisk the pudding to incorporate any liquid on top and break up the chia seeds, then spoon pudding into bowls. Top with the popped amaranth, mint sprigs, and berries.

Sign-up Now
and Be Notified of New Books

Website: readbooks.today

Printed in Great Britain
by Amazon

53059587R00042